BUTTERFLY GA

How to encourage butt visit and breed in your

C000245808

Contents

Tables

With many thanks to Anne and Gibby for all their support

The Garden Butterfly Year

The table shows the main months when you are most likely to see the commonest garden butterflies. The time period will vary depending on where in the country you are situated and the weather conditions, and butterflies will sometimes be seen outside these times.

Species	J	F	M	A	M	J	J	A	S	O	N	D
Brimstone			🦋	🦋	🦋	🦋	🦋	🦋	🦋			
Clouded yellow							🦋	🦋				
Comma			🦋	🦋			🦋	🦋				
Common blue					🦋	🦋		🦋	🦋			
Essex skipper							🦋	🦋				
Gatekeeper							🦋	🦋				
Green hairstreak					🦋	🦋						
Green-veined white					🦋	🦋	🦋	🦋				
Holly blue				🦋	🦋		🦋	🦋				
Large skipper						🦋	🦋	🦋				
Large white					🦋	🦋	🦋	🦋				
Marbled white						🦋	🦋	🦋				
Meadow brown						🦋	🦋	🦋				
Orange tip				🦋	🦋	🦋						
Painted lady						🦋	🦋	🦋	🦋			
Peacock			🦋	🦋			🦋	🦋	🦋			
Red admiral					🦋	🦋	🦋	🦋	🦋	🦋		
Ringlet						🦋	🦋					
Small copper					🦋	🦋	🦋					
Small skipper							🦋	🦋				
Small tortoiseshell					🦋	🦋	🦋	🦋	🦋			
Small white					🦋	🦋	🦋	🦋	🦋			
Speckled wood					🦋	🦋	🦋	🦋	🦋			
Wall brown					🦋	🦋	🦋	🦋				

ONE
Introduction

Why encourage butterflies to the garden?

To some traditional gardeners the idea of actively encouraging butterflies into the garden might seem rather strange. Most vegetable growers associate butterflies with holes in their cabbage leaves as the rather pretty green caterpillars of the large white and small white butterflies munch their way into all members of the Brassica family – cauliflowers, Brussells sprouts, broccoli and of course cabbages of all shapes and sizes. Yet if they are given the opportunity to learn a little more about our native butterflies, many gardeners become keen to actively encourage all species, including the dreaded 'cabbage whites'.

So what value do butterflies have in our gardens? The easy answer to that question is 'not much', although a few do pollinate some flowers for us and it could be argued that caterpillars recycle plant material. But butterflies are important in many other ways. If lots of butterflies, both species and individuals, are present in our environment it is usually an indication that there is a great variety of other creatures present also, and the environment is relatively healthy. A lack of butterflies means a lack of biodiversity generally and we are all poorer for it.

For many people the presence of butterflies in their garden is simply a pleasure in itself. All our native species are beautiful insects displaying colours ranging from bright red (red admiral, small tortoiseshell) to shades of blue (common and holly blue) and green (green hairstreak). To walk through the garden in the summer and see a cloud of small tortoiseshells lift from a Buddleia bush, is one of the joys of gardening.

Why have butterflies declined in our countryside?

Of course another reason for encouraging butterflies to our gardens is that they have declined dramatically in the wild. There are many reasons for this and the organisation Butterfly Conservation has studied this aspect of butterfly ecology. Their research shows that as a result of the loss of habitats such as hedgerows and hay meadows, the actual numbers of some species, for instance the pretty common blue and speckled wood, have declined by as much as 70 per cent in the last 100 years. Many of these once common butterflies are adapting to live in our gardens and if the conditions are right will visit and breed in this new habitat. Thus gardens are becoming increasingly important in the conservation of some species of butterfly, although there are of course several species that will not readily adapt to garden situations. Having said that, we can do a great deal to encourage the ones that will.

Are some species increasing? What are the effects of climate change?

Although in general our native butterflies are decreasing in actual numbers, for some their range is increasing as a result of our climate warming. Examples are the comma, orange tip and brimstone butterflies, whose range has increased northwards over the last 20 years. There is a fairly marked north-south divide where our butterfly species are concerned, and several of the species that are common in the south of the country are rarely seen in the north. There is very little we can do about this fact of nature, but the knowledge that some are extending their range is good news for those of us who live in the north of the country. However we must balance this against the general overall loss of numbers throughout the country as a whole. Also, butterflies such as the red admiral which migrates to our shores in early summer, are arriving earlier. Sadly the overall result is still a depressing realisation that loss of habitat, intensive farming and the widespread use of pesticides have all contributed to the decimation of our native butterfly population.

What sort of garden will they visit?

Butterflies are relatively mobile insects and will visit any garden, however small. But that visit will be fleeting if there is nothing there to tempt them to stay around, and that doesn't mean just the plants that provide the adult insects with nectar. We must also take into account the requirements needed by their caterpillars (the plants they feed on, and the shelter they require) and for those species that hibernate in this country, the conditions they need to survive the winter. Chapter 2 will give you some idea of the complicated life cycle of the butterfly and how we can provide for all these different stages in a garden environment, and Chapter 3 shows you how to make your garden more butterfly friendly. So no matter how small your garden, it is possible to make it into a butterfly haven and by doing so you will also be encouraging lots of other wildlife as well.

How many butterflies can you expect?

This depends on many factors, the most important being your location and the habitats round about you. I have a friend whose garden backs onto woodland, and fritillaries, white admirals and even purple emperors have appeared in her garden. My own garden is surrounded by other (generally wildlife-unfriendly) gardens, and on one short border by arable farmland, with no good butterfly habitats for miles around. This meant that initially it attracted only a few common species, but was all the more exciting and challenging a space to work with because of that. Within just three or four years, 24 species had been recorded entirely as a result of making sure that the butterflies' requirements were met. But it does pay to be realistic – however much I would love to see a white admiral in my tiny woodland area, it is very unlikely to happen in spite of planting the caterpillar food plant for this species – wild honeysuckle. With no habitat nearby where this gorgeous butterfly can be found, I could only expect a wandering, lost individual – and that's very unlikely to happen!

Most gardens, even quite small ones in built up areas, are quite capable of attracting between 10 and 15 butterfly species. These insects have an amazing ability to search out the nectar plants they require, and if you grow the right plants and have the right conditions for them, they will find your garden eventually. And the more types of nectar-producing plants you grow, the more species of butterfly you are likely to attract. A national survey of butterflies in gardens carried out by members of Butterfly Conservation showed that in order to attract the maximum number of butterfly species, it was crucial to grow at least 30 different nectar plants. If you are fortunate enough to have a larger garden with room for plenty of nectar plants, particularly if you live in a more rural area, you may easily attract over 20 species.

There are five species of butterfly that appear in even the smallest wildlife-friendly garden. They are the small and large whites (often called the cabbage whites), the small tortoiseshell, red admiral and peacock. These are familiar insects to most gardeners - however it is still easy to confuse the whites. The inside back cover of this book has recommendations of useful books for the identification of butterflies – essential if you want to keep records of the insects you see and identify them correctly. It is also wise to know a little about the timing of the emergence of certain species. Most butterflies will only be seen at certain times throughout the year and this fact will help with their identification. Page 2 has information on the Garden Butterfly Year.

As well as the common five, some gardens may also have the beautiful brimstone, the holly and common blues, painted lady, comma, some of the 'browns', orange tip and green-veined white. There is more information about these species in Chapter 2.

Can you introduce butterflies to your garden?
I am sometimes asked whether it is a good idea to introduce wildlife to gardens. It is possible to buy the eggs or pupae of British butterfly species, and this may seem like a good idea if butterflies are scarce in your area. However, if butterflies are seen infrequently, it means that the conditions they require to thrive are just not available, and there is a good chance that by introducing them you would simply be condemning them to a very short life with little chance of reproducing. It is much better to concentrate on changing those conditions, building up the habitat they

require in your garden and let nature take its course.

Rearing butterflies from caterpillars though can be a useful and fascinating exercise for small children. A 'cabbage' white caterpillar or two from the garden, looked after with care and reared through pupation to adult emergence, can be an excellent and exciting way for children to learn not just about the life cycle of these fascinating insects, but also about the environment and ecology in general.

TWO
Garden Butterflies and their Life Cycles

The butterfly life cycle

All of us know what an adult butterfly looks like but understanding their life cycles can make a huge difference to how we manage our gardens to accommodate and encourage these insects. Once I realised that the tiny caterpillar of the common blue, one of my favourite butterflies, spends the winter months down in the bottom of tussocks of grass, I thought again about how short I cut my garden meadow areas where I knew the common blue was breeding. Several other species of butterfly spend the winter in their caterpillar stage, including the small and large skippers. Some such as the large and small whites, over-winter as pupae, and other species, in particular the brimstone, peacock, small tortoiseshell and comma hibernate as adults. It is very important that we take these factors into consideration when making our gardens butterfly friendly and there is more information on how to do this in Chapter 3.

The life cycle of the butterfly is something we all learn about as children. The adult butterflies mate and the female lays her eggs on larval (caterpillar) food plants, detecting them by scent. These caterpillar food plants are very specific to each species – some butterflies will use only one type of plant. For example the white admiral lays her eggs on wild honeysuckle, and the small tortoiseshell caterpillar will eat only nettles and nothing else. Other species are a little more adaptable – the female comma will lay her eggs on the leaves of hops, nettles, elm trees or occasionally other tree species. Once the caterpillar has fed and grown to reach its optimum size, it will pupate. The pupa or chrysalis is tucked away out of harm perhaps on a plant stem, beneath a leaf or if the butterfly is a species that spends the winter as a pupa, this may be attached to a fence or wall. When the transformation to adult butterfly has taken place two or three weeks later, (or several months later if it spends the winter as a pupa), the adult insect will emerge with limp folded wings. Over the next few minutes the wings will be inflated with fluid, allowed to stiffen and dry out in the sunshine over an hour or so, and the butterfly will be off to find a mate and start the life cycle over again.

Migration

One other point we must consider is that not all of our butterflies spend their whole lives in Britain. Some migrate from warmer places, and visit us to breed in the summer, just like many species of bird. Examples of migrating butterflies are the red admiral and painted lady. These generally do not survive the winter with us, but at least some of them return to the Continent each autumn.

Why are native plants important to butterflies?
Our native wildflowers, trees, shrubs and climbers are of great importance to all our native wildlife. These, generally, are the plants upon which they depend for food – a relationship that has built up over many thousands of years. It stands to reason therefore, that the more native plants you have in your garden, the more wildlife you will attract. Where breeding butterflies are concerned, this is certainly the case. However, when we look at providing nectar for the adult insects, rather than food for their caterpillars, there are many non-native plants that are excellent sources of energy-giving nectar. We will be looking at some of these plants in Chapter 4. But if you are looking at more than just supplying butterflies with a place to stock up on nectar and would like to provide a habitat for them to establish a breeding colony, you will need to consider growing their larval food plants. You will find more information on that aspect of butterfly gardening in Chapter 5.

What about moths?
A quick word here about moths – the poor relations of butterflies. Many people find moths unpleasant. They flutter around lights at night and we often have little more than a fleeting glimpse of what seem to be dull brown insects. But many moths are stunningly beautiful – even more beautiful than some butterflies. Once you get hooked on attracting butterflies to your garden, there is every chance that moths will become a fascination too. Growing native plants will benefit these insects immensely as the majority of moth caterpillars feed on the leaves of wild flowers and shrubs. For more information on moths, turn to the book list on the inside back cover.

Our commonest garden butterflies
The five species of butterfly that appear in most gardens are described below in order of their abundance. Another seven or eight are also relatively common and will put in an appearance if they can find a good source of nectar.

Small tortoiseshell *Aglais urticae*
The small tortoiseshell is the butterfly you are most likely to see in your garden and one of the easiest to attract. With its orange and black markings and pretty blue edge to the wings, it is also easy to identify. In the south of the country there are usually two generations each year, but only one in the north. The adults emerge from

A wildlife garden area with plants to attract butterflies and moths

Small tortoiseshell butterfly on
Sedum Frosty Morn

Painted lady taking nectar
from field scabious

A male orange tip on honesty flowers

Brimstone butterfly feeding on
Michaelmas daisy

Meadow cranesbill with
small skipper

Speckled wood on white Sedum

Ringlet - a less common
garden visitor

A marbled white resting on lavender

A garden meadow ideal for butterflies

hibernation in late March or April, immediately mate and the female lays her eggs on fresh nettle leaves in full sun. The caterpillars are black, mottled with tiny white spots, and have two yellow stripes along each side. They also have black spines along their backs, and are usually found in large numbers within a silky tent. After pupation the adults emerge in July and feed avidly on a variety of plants including the wild scabious species, Phuopsis, dandelion, thyme and mint. The life cycle is repeated in the south of the country, and the second brood of butterflies feeds on ice plant, Buddleia, Hebe, fleabane and Michaelmas daisy, before finding a place to hibernate.

Large and Small White *Pieris brassicae and Pieris rapae*

Both these species are known as cabbage whites, for obvious reasons. The bane of many gardeners, they are really quite delicate and beautiful. The wings of the large white have black tips and several black spots, and this butterfly can be seen at almost any time, in varying numbers throughout the spring and summer. Its main seasons are May and then July and August when our native bred insects are joined by an influx of adults from the Continent. The large white lays her eggs in groups on the undersides of the leaves of any of the cabbage family, but the green caterpillars will also eat the leaves of nasturtiums. If these plants are grown near the vegetable garden, the female large white will often choose the nasturtium leaves rather than those of cabbages and cauliflowers. The adult butterflies enjoy the nectar from catmint, runner beans, hyssop, lavender, Buddleia and Aubretia and the second brood over-winter as pupae. The small white is very similar in appearance to the large, but is distinctly smaller and the black markings are paler. They are seen mainly between April and May and again between July and September, but like the large white may be seen at any time throughout the summer. The female lays her eggs singly on the undersides of cabbage leaves, and the pale green caterpillars are well camouflaged whilst feeding. The adults prefer nectar from lavender, Aubretia and catmint.

Peacock *Inachis io*

The peacock is one of our most familiar butterflies, being mainly red with large eye spots like those on a peacock's tail. Like the small tortoiseshell it uses nettle leaves as its caterpillar food plant. Clusters of eggs are laid on plants in full sun and the caterpillars that emerge are black and spiky. The adults that have survived hibernation are on the wing in April and May, and the single brood of new adults can be seen in gardens in July and August. These are the individuals that go on to hibernate through the winter. The peacock has a strong preference for the nectar from Buddleia, but also likes dandelion, hemp agrimony and Michaelmas daisy.

Red Admiral *Vanessa atalanta*
The red admiral is a stunning butterfly, its wings being almost black with red stripes and white markings on the tips. Very few survive the winter with us, and those we see in the late spring have usually migrated across the Channel from the Continent. On arrival the adults mate and the female lays her eggs singly on nettle leaves. The dark grey to black caterpillar is spiky, with a few yellowish spots, and feeds and pupates inside a small shelter made by sticking the edges of the nettle leaves together with silk. The summer butterflies love Buddleia as a nectar source, but those that are around in the autumn are especially fond of Michaelmas daisies and the flowers of ivy. This is also a butterfly that will take the juice from rotten fruit, particularly plums.

As well as these five species, most people can expect to see several other species in even quite a small garden. These are described below.

Brimstone *Gonepteryx rhamni*
This is a familiar butterfly to most of us, although the female may be mistaken for a large white, as her wings do not have the sulphur yellow colour of the male. However, the distinctive wavy edge to the wing distinguishes her from this more common species. The brimstone is the longest lived of all our native butterflies, surviving up to nine months, but occurs only in the southern half of the country. Its distribution is strongly reflected in the availability of its caterpillar food plants, two species of the small buckthorn shrub. The adults will fly long distances to find the plant, attracted by its scent. This is usually one of the first butterflies out of hibernation on warm days in March or even February. The green caterpillars are very well camouflaged on the leaves of buckthorn and after pupation the adult insects emerge in mid-summer. These individuals spend the summer and autumn months feeding on a variety of plants, especially brightly coloured flowers such as broad leaved everlasting pea, runner bean, knapweed and Buddleia. This butterfly has a particularly long tongue and can take nectar from plants that other species cannot reach. These same adults hibernate through the winter months, and emerge in the early spring.

Comma *Polygonia c-album*
The comma is a southern butterfly and is the only mainly orange coloured butterfly that commonly visits gardens, making it relatively easy to identify. However it is quite a fast flyer, easily disturbed, and does not always obligingly stay still! However, when you do see it well there is no mistaking the scalloped wing edges, which give the closed wings the appearance of dried leaves, and the white comma shaped mark on the wing underside. The adult butterflies hibernate and emerge in spring to lay their

eggs on nettles or hops. The caterpillars are not like their small tortoiseshell relatives in appearance, but are pale in colour with spines and orange markings. They pupate to produce the summer brood of adult insects which are often more brightly coloured than the spring individuals. The summer butterflies nectar on Buddleia and Michaelmas daisy and like red admirals, enjoy the juices from rotting fruit. This butterfly is strongly territorial and will defend its corner vigorously, sometimes flying at any passing intruder, including the garden owner!

Common Blue *Polyommatus icarus*
The appearance of this beautiful little butterfly can be confusing to the amateur as the colours of both male and female are variable. The two sexes are also quite different from each other. The male is bright blue with a white margin to the upper side of his wings, but the female may be blue or brown with small orange spots along the edges of her wings. However, most blue butterflies in gardens in mid summer are likely to be common blues, which helps with identification. This species can be encouraged into gardens by growing its preferred larval food plant, the common bird's foot trefoil, and a few of its favourite nectar plants, especially marjoram and cornflower. In the south this species usually has two broods a year, the first adults appearing in late May. They have spent the winter as tiny caterpillars, completing their growth in the spring before pupating. On cool evenings the common blue can sometimes be seen roosting high up on tall grass stems. This tiny butterfly is very rarely seen on Buddleia but as well as marjoram and cornflower, it will take nectar from the bird's foot trefoil flowers and the wildflower common fleabane.

Gatekeeper *Pyronia tithonus*
Gatekeepers are sometimes abundant in gardens, especially those with a meadow area and some wild marjoram, the favourite nectar plant of this little butterfly. The upper wings are orange with pale brown margins and there is a prominent eyespot on the tip of the forewing. The butterfly gets the name gatekeeper, and its alternative name of hedge brown, from its habit in the wild of patrolling hedges and gateways, where bramble flowers, another favourite nectar source are found. It is quite territorial and males will fight with each other to secure a breeding spot. There is only one brood per year, and the first adult butterflies are seen in July. Eggs are laid on a variety of native grasses, and the tiny caterpillars feed until October, when they retreat to the depths of the grass tussocks and hibernate until the spring, until they are fully grown in June. Pupation then takes place and the adults emerge in July. Gatekeepers love the flowers of marjoram and this plant alone will keep them happy if they are around your garden.

Green-veined White *Pieris napi*

The green-veined white is rather more like the orange tip than the cabbage whites in its habits and preferences. It can be distinguished from the large and small whites by the presence of slightly fuzzy grey lines along either side of the veins, on the underside of the wings. It lays its eggs singly on garlic mustard and lady's smock and the green caterpillar is not easy to find. The adult butterflies are around in May and June, and again in July and August when the second brood appears. These adults mate and lay eggs, the caterpillars pupate and they then spend the winter in the pupal stage, emerging in late April and May. Like the orange tip, this butterfly takes nectar from the flowers of Aubretia, honesty and sweet rocket, and will also visit candytuft.

Holly Blue *Celastrina argiolus*

This strong flying little blue butterfly is found only in the south of the country and is most likely to be seen in your garden if you have holly and ivy, its two larval food plants, nearby. It is a species that has good and bad years in terms of its numbers, and this natural cycle is thought to come about as a result of the presence of a parasitic wasp, which preys on the holly blue caterpillars. Although the wasp clearly plays a part in the fortunes of this small butterfly, it is likely that there are other factors involved. There are two broods each year, and the first holly blues are generally seen in April. These mate and lay their eggs on the tiny developing flowers of holly or occasionally the native shrub dogwood, which the caterpillars then eat. After pupation a second brood appears in July and August. These adults lay their eggs on the flowers of mature ivy and the tiny bright blue butterflies can sometimes be seen, flying high up around the tops of trees or walls where the ivy flowers are situated. The caterpillars that result from this brood pupate and spend the winter in this state, ready to emerge in the spring sunshine. Holly blues take nectar from rather limited sources, but marjoram and forget-me-not are useful, as are the flowers of ivy. The adult butterfly is sometimes confused with the common blue, but unlike that species has fewer markings on the undersides of the wings, which are pale blue with small black spots.

Orange Tip *Anthocharis cardamines*

This beautiful butterfly lives up to its common name, as the male has bright orange tips to the ends of its forewings. We see mainly one brood a year, between April and June and it is a relatively easy butterfly to attract to the garden if the right plants are grown but we never see it in large numbers. Both orange-tipped males and white females have mottled green undersides to their wings, making them easy to identify when they are at rest or nectaring on their favourite plants. Although the traditional habitat of this species, the wet meadow, is declining, it is adapting to roadsides and gardens, where it finds alternative larval food plants to the lady's smock (cuckoo flower) that has always been the main species on which it lays its eggs. In these situations other species, especially garlic mustard, sweet rocket and honesty are used. The eggs are laid singly amongst the flower stems where the caterpillar is well camouflaged, as it closely resembles a tiny seed pod. It pupates in the summer and spends the next eight or nine months in this state, deep down the vegetation, until the adult insect emerges in the spring. Orange tips feed on the flowers on which they lay their eggs, so growing honesty, sweet rocket, garlic mustard and also Aubretia will attract them.

Painted Lady *Cynthia cardui*

This is another migrant butterfly that reaches our shores in spring and summer, sometimes in huge numbers. It travels from North Africa across the Continent, making its way as far north as Scotland in good years. The adult butterfly is pale orange with black and white markings on the wings, and is very attracted to Buddleia. Once the spring adults have arrived, they mate and lay their eggs on thistles, although occasionally nettles and mallow are used. The black spiky caterpillars feed inside a tent of leaves, held together with silky threads. After pupation these adults emerge in mid summer and mingle with more African migrants which sometimes arrive in huge numbers, as they did in 1996 when there was an enormous influx of these beautiful butterflies. These insects breed again, and after emergence the butterflies feed on a variety of nectar plants including Buddleia, scabious and statice until late summer when they return south. Those that do not return sadly die, as they are not capable of surviving our winters.

Other butterfly species

You may be lucky and have other species of butterfly such as skippers or browns visiting your garden. Throughout the rest of this book, nectar plants and larval food plants of some of the less common species that visit and breed in gardens, are mentioned and the months in which they appear are included in The Garden Butterfly Year on Page 2.

THREE
Making your Garden Butterfly Friendly

We have already seen how fussy butterflies can be where their preferences for their caterpillar food plants and nectar sources are concerned. This is not actually fussiness of course, but the result of many thousands of years of evolution that have determined the place of each species in the habitat they occupy. In the same way, they have evolved to take advantage of other factors in their environment, and in order to give them the conditions they require we need to look at the situations in which they thrive.

Gardeners who live in the north may already be feeling a little disappointed, because it is becoming clear that the natural range of many species does not extend throughout the country. Most butterflies prefer warm conditions and are not fond of cold, windswept locations. This brings us to the first important factor that we need to consider when adapting our gardens as butterfly habitats.

Shelter
When I first began to count the butterfly species in my newly acquired garden, then a very open space with small pruned fruit trees (the area had been part of a commercial orchard), there were only six or seven butterfly species regularly seen during the summer months. In spite of the small trees the area was windswept across open fields from the north and east, and it was quite inhospitable to these insects. My first task was to plant a mixed native hedge around the whole garden, and also to allow the fruit trees to grow and fill out. There was less fruit, but a much more sheltered environment was created. Within four years the butterfly count was up into the twenties, and rose to twenty-four species quite soon after that. The shelter the hedge provided as it grew, along with the provision of larval food plants and good nectar producing species, made an enormous difference in a very short time. That shelter though was crucial, because butterflies will not hang around if your garden is windy and unwelcoming, however many good nectar plants you have.

Butterflies are cold-blooded insects and need the warmth of the sun to coax them into activity early in the day. They often bask in the sun's warmth first thing in the morning – this is why making warm sheltered spots in the garden is so vital, especially in spring and autumn, when the sun is lower and less of the garden receives its natural warmth. On a sunny day butterflies like the same conditions that we do – full sun and out of the wind! If your garden is very open in its aspect it will

Butterfly Nectar Plants - Native Wildflowers

Top 20 for gardens are highlighted

Wildflower	Colour/Flowering Time:	Add to:	Favourite nectar source:
Betony	Pink/June-October	Border, meadow	Brimstone
Bird's foot trefoil	Yellow/June-September	Border, container, meadow	Common blue
Bluebell	Blue/April-June	Shady border or grass	Large white
Bramble	White/May-November	Hedgerow, wild patch	Many species
Broad leaved pea	Pink/July-August	Border, patio	Brimstone
Bugle	Purple/April-June	Border, pond edge, container	Whites
Burdock	Pink/July-September	Wild patch	Peacock, small tortoiseshell
Common fleabane	Yellow/August-September	Border, pond edge	Many species
Common knapweed	Purple/June-September	Meadow	Many species
Common valerian	Pink/June-August	Border, pond edge	Small tortoiseshell
Cornflower	Blue/June-August	Border, container	Common blue, gatekeeper
Corn marigold	Yellow/June-September	Border, container	Skippers
Creeping thistle	Purple/June-September	Wild patch	Small tortoiseshell
Creeping thyme	Pink/May-August	Border, container	Many species
Dandelion	Yellow/March-October	Meadow	Many species
Field scabious	Mauve/June-August	Border, meadow	Many species
Garlic mustard	White/April-June	Border, shady grass	Orange tip, green veined white
Greater bird's foot trefoil	Yellow/June-August	Pond edge, container	Common blue
Greater knapweed	Purple/July-September	Border, meadow	Many species
Hedge cranesbill	Mauve/June-August	Border, meadow	Brimstone
Hemp agrimony	Pink/July-September	Border, pond edge	Many species
Horseshoe vetch	Yellow/April-July	Border, container	Common blue
Ivy	White/September-November	Border	Red admiral, comma
Kidney vetch	Yellow/June-September	Border, container	Common blue
Lady's smock	Mauve/April-June	Border, meadow	Green veined white, orange tip
Lesser burdock	Purple/July-September	Wild patch	Peacock, brimstone
Meadow cranesbill	Blue/June-September	Border, meadow	Small tortoiseshell, skippers
Ox eye daisy	White/May-September	Border, meadow, container	Many species
Primrose	Yellow/March-April	Border, container	Small tortoiseshell, brimstone
Purple loosestrife	Purple/July-September	Border, pond edge	Whites
Ragged robin	Pink/May-August	Border, meadow, pond edge	Whites
Rockrose	Yellow/June-September	Border, container	Blues
Scotch thistle	Purple/July-September	Border, wild patch	Small tortoiseshell
Sheep's bit	Mauve/May-August	Border, container	Many species
Small scabious	Mauve/July-August	Border, container	Many species
Teasel	Pink/July-August	Border, wild patch	Many species
Thrift	Pink/April-August	Border, container	Small tortoiseshell
Vervain	Vervain/June-October	Border, wild patch	Whites
Viper's bugloss	Purple/June-September	Border, wild patch	Skippers
Water mint	Pink/July-September	Pond edge, container	Many species
Wild basil	Pink/July-September	Meadow, container	Whites
Wild marjoram	Pink/July-September	Border, meadow, container	Many species
Yarrow	White/July-October	Meadow, wild patch	Meadow brown, ringlet

Many species - where more than 3 species are attracted to a particular plant

Butterfly Nectar Plants - Perennials

The plants listed here are particularly good at attracting large numbers of insects to their nectar. The best are highlighted.

Perennials	Colour/Flowering Time:	Best species/varieties	Favourite nectar source:
Aster	Various/Summer	A. alpinus	
Aubretia	Mauve, pink/Spring	Single varieties	Many species
Catmint	Blue/Summer	Six Hills Giant	Whites
Chives	Pink/Summer		
Chrysanthemum	Various/Late Summer	Korean types, single varieties	Red admiral, small tortoiseshell
Coneflower	Pink, white/Late Summer	Any	Red admiral
Coreopsis	Yellow/Summer		
Cornflower	Blue, purple/Summer	Centaurea species	Many species
Cranesbill	Various/Early Summer	Single varieties	Skippers
Elecampagne	Yellow/Summer		
Fleabone	Pink, mauve/Summer	Erigeron varieties	Small tortoiseshell
Globe thistle	Blue/Summer		
Grape hyacinth	Blue/Spring		Peacock
Heather	Pink, purple/Summer		Comma, small copper
Hyssop	Blue, white/Summer		Whites
Ice plant	Pink, white/Late Summer	Pale colours only	Many species
Knapweed	Pink, purple/Summer	Centaurea dealbata	
Lavender	Purple/Summer	Any varieties including dwarf	Many species
Lychnis	Pink, white/Summer	Lychnis coronaria	
Marjoram	Pink/Summer	Any	Many species
Michaelmas daisy	Various/Late Summer	Single, pale varieties	Many species
Mint	Pink/Summer	Any	Many species
Onion	Various/Summer	Allium species	
Pearl everlasting	White/Summer		Small tortoiseshell, gatekeeper
Phlox	Various/Summer	P. paniculata, pale colours	Many species
Phuopsis	Pink/Summer		Small tortoiseshell
Runner bean	Red, white/Summer		Whites, brimstone
Scabious	Various/Summer	Any	Many species
Sea holly	Blue/Summer		
Shasta daisy	White/Summer		Small tortoiseshell
Sneezeweed	Various/Late Summer	Helenium species	Red admiral
Stock	Various/Summer	Matthiola species	
Thyme	Pink/Summer	Any	Many species
Tobacco plant	Various/Summer	Sensation Mixed	
Valerian	Pink, white, red/Summer	Pink and white varieties	Many species
Verbena	Various/Summer	V. bonariensis	Red admiral
Wallflower	Various/Summer	Bowles mauve	Whites
Yarrow	Various/Summer	Pink and mauve	Browns

Many species - where more than 3 species are attracted to a particular plant

Annuals and Biennials

Annuals/Biennials	Colour/Flowering Time:	Best species/varieties	Favourite nectar source:
Ageratum	Blue/Summer		
Alyssum	Various/Summer	Royal Carpet, Rosie O'Day	
Candytuft	Various/Summer	Pale colours	Many species
Cornflower	Various/Summer	Any	Many species
Cosmos	Various/Late Summer	Early Sensation mixed	Many species
Dahlia	Various/Late Summer	Single varieties, Coltness, Redskin	Painted lady
Everlasting flower	Various/Summer	Any everlastings	Many species
Forget-me-not	Blue/Late Spring	Any	Many species
French marigold	Yellow, orange/Summer	Marietta and Spanish Brocade	Many species
Heliotrope	Purple/Late Summer		Many species
Honesty	Purple, white/Late Spring		Many species
Lobelia	Blue, white/Summer	Any	Many species
Petunia	Various/Summer	Blue or white single varieties	
Scabious	Various/Summer	Any	Many species
Statice	Various/Summer	Any	Painted lady
Sweet rocket	Mauve, white/Late Spring		Many species
Sweet william	Various/Late Spring	Pale colours	Skippers
Sunflower	Yellow/Late Summer	Avoid very double types	Many species
Verbena	Various/Summer	Pale colours	Red admiral
Wallflower	Various/Late Spring	Pale colours	Whites

Shrubs

Shrubs	Colour/Flowering Time:	Best species/varieties	Favourite nectar source:
Buddleia alternifolia	Mauve/Summer		Many species
Buddleia davidii	Mauve, white/Summer	Pale colours especially Lochinch	Many species
Buddleia weyeriana	Yellow/July-November	Any	Many species
Ceratostigma	Blue/Late Summer		
Cotoneaster	White/Late Spring		Red admiral
Escallonia	Various/Summer	White varieties	Holly blue
Goat willow	Yellow/Spring		Small tortoiseshell, peacock
Hebe	Pale colours/Summer-Autumn	Pink varieties, Great Orme	Many species
Lilac	White, mauve/Summer	Single varieties	
Privet	White/Summer	Wild species	Many species
Wild plum	White/Spring		Peacock, small tortoiseshell

Many species - where more than 3 species are attracted to a particular plant

The Larval Food Plants of Garden Butterflies

Species	Larval Food Plants	Location in the Garden
Brimstone	Buckthorn	Border, hedgerow
Comma	Nettles, hops, elm	Container, wild patch
Common blue	Bird's foot trefoil, restharrow, black medick	Border, meadow, container
Essex skipper	Native grasses, especially cock's-foot	Meadow, wild patch
Gatekeeper	Native grasses, especially meadow grasses, fescues, cock's-foot, bents	Meadow, wild patch
Green-veined white	Garlic mustard, sweet rocket*, lady's smock	Border, meadow
Holly blue	Holly, ivy, dogwood	Hedgerow
Large skipper	Native grasses, especially cock's-foot, false brome	Meadow, wild patch
Large white	All brassica species (cabbages), Nasturtiums*	Border, container
Marbled white	Native grasses, especially fescues, cock's-foot	Meadow, wild patch
Meadow brown	Native grasses, especially meadow grasses, bents	Meadow, wild patch
Orange tip	Garlic mustard, sweet rocket*, lady's smock, honesty*	Border, meadow
Painted lady	Thistles, mallow	Container, wild patch
Peacock	Nettles	Container, wild patch
Red admiral	Nettles	Container, wild patch
Ringlet	Native grasses, especially cock's-foot, Timothy grass and false brome	Meadow, wild patch
Small copper	Wild sorrel	Border, meadow, container
Small heath	Fescues and meadow grass	Meadow, wild patch
Small skipper	Native grasses, especially Yorkshire fog, Timothy grass and false brome	Meadow, wild patch
Small tortoisehell	Nettles	Container, wild patch
Small white	All Brassica species, Nasturtiums*	Border, container
Speckled wood	Native grasses, especially cock's-foot, meadow grass, false brome, couch grass	Meadow, wild patch
Wall brown	Native grasses, especially cock's-foot, common bent, Yorkshire fog	Meadow, wild patch

* non-native plants

Some Meadow Grasses used by Butterflies

Bents	Agrostis species
Cock's-foot	Dactylis glomerata
Couch	Elymus species
False brome	Brachypodium sylvaticum
Fescue	Festuca species
Meadow grass	Poa species
Timothy	Phleum pratense
Tor grass	Brachypodium pinnatum
Yorkshire fog	Holcus lanatus

be worthwhile planting a few well positioned shrubs or a good hedge, and making sure that fences are well maintained and gap free. Traditional hedging such as privet or the much maligned Leyland cypress (as long as it is diligently pruned to keep it thick and under control) is fine. But if you have space and would like the hedge to be a real feature, then a mixed native hedge will provide food and shelter, not just for butterflies but lots of other wildlife as well.

Planting a hedge for butterflies

Native hedging is best planted in the late autumn or winter, and the small shrubs can generally be bought 'bare-rooted', that is, not in pots, but dug straight out of their nursery beds. This makes them very reasonably priced, but has the disadvantage that they must be planted as soon as you have bought them or 'heeled in' somewhere in the garden until you have time to plant them. The panel below has some suggestions for hedging plants that are particularly valuable to butterflies and are suitable for most soil types. They should be planted into good soil, watered well and mulched to maintain the soil moisture. You may need to continue to water for at least their first spring and summer, especially if the weather is dry. Plant about 45 cms apart and if you have room for a double row, your hedge will be even thicker and more wildlife friendly, providing a good habitat for small mammals and birds as well as butterflies. Before planting you can remove about one third of the top growth of the small shrubs if you wish. This will encourage them to bush out thickly from the base.

Native shrubs for a butterfly hedge:

Blackthorn	*Prunus spinosa*	Nectar for early small tortoiseshell and peacock
Buckthorn	*Frangula alnus or Rhamnus catharticus*	Larval food plant of brimstone
Dogwood	*Cornus sanguinea*	Alternative larval food plant for holly blue
Goat Willow	*Salix capraea*	Nectar for early small tortoiseshell and peacock. Excellent for moths
Hawthorn	*Crataegus monogyna*	Good shelter and food for wildlife
Holly	*Ilex aquifolia*	Excellent shelter, and larval food plant of holly blue
Wild Plum	*Prunus sp*	Nectar for early small tortoiseshell and peacock
Wild Privet	*Ligustrum vulgare*	Good nectar source for many butterflies and moths

It is important that a native hedge is allowed to flower, as some of the plants provide nectar for early spring butterflies just out of hibernation, but this does not mean that it has to become enormous. Once it is established it can be pruned with care in the autumn, by taking out any long leading shoots, but leaving berries. Maintain it at a height of two meters if you are short of space or light. After ten years of rather slow growth, our native hedges are now laid in the traditional Midland style. This means they continue to flower and produce berries for wildlife, and they stay nice and thick at the bottom, making them ideal shelter for small mammals such as hedgehogs. They also encourage many nesting birds as well as keep the cold spring winds at bay.

Shelter does not have to be provided in the form of a native hedge of course. You may choose to use non-native shrubs which encourage butterflies and other wildlife. Buddleias are not terribly suitable on their own as they tend to become open and straggly, but a mixture of holly, Pyracantha, Berberis, Viburnum tinus and Escallonia will make a thick butterfly friendly hedge, with flowers and berries for other wildlife. Include a Buddleia too and cut it back hard each spring to encourage flowering shoots and try to include the native buckthorn to attract breeding brimstones. If you can add a few climbers like hop, everlasting pea and honeysuckle you will enhance the hedge further, both in terms of its appearance and its wildlife friendly nature.

Even if your garden is relatively sheltered, or you have decided to plant a hedge or adapt existing features to make it so, you still need to consider some other important factors. The most crucial of these is the use of chemicals in the garden.

Pesticides

If you are not currently gardening organically, you will need to consider this approach if you really want to create a butterfly haven. Pesticides are designed to kill insects – it is as simple as that. Even those that target specific types of insect such as aphids, will have a knock on effect on all the wildlife in your garden, which is undesirable. Aphids are a very important source of food for many small birds like tits and wrens, so their extermination from your garden will deny these birds quite a large percentage of their normal diet. These same pesticides may kill caterpillars and without caterpillars, we have no butterflies!

Gardening without pesticides can seem quite daunting when you first begin, but the fear that you will be overwhelmed by undesirable insects soon disappears. As a natural balance between pest and predator builds up, it is unlikely that you will get an unhealthy increase of one particular creature. If this does start to happen, the other wildlife that uses it for food will also increase in number, and the balance is restored. It is only when we take one factor out of this equation that everything starts to become unbalanced. If the caterpillars of butterflies do get out of hand, and this only ever happens with the large and small whites, there are other ways of dealing with them. They can be removed by hand and even put onto the bird table if you wish, where tits and robins will find them. This is what happens to lots of them naturally anyway, but is maybe not for the squeamish! Growing nasturtiums nearby, as we have already seen, gives the adult large and small white butterflies an alternative food plant on which to lay their eggs. If your cabbages and cauliflowers really do suffer, cover them with fleece when you see the first adult whites flying in the springtime, to provide a physical barrier to prevent them depositing their eggs.

All the other common garden butterflies lay their eggs on plants such as nettles, honesty, sweet rocket, wild sorrel, garlic mustard and other wildflowers or grasses (see Chapter 5 for more information on this) and we really don't notice any damage from the caterpillars. In fact, the majority of butterfly larvae are very difficult to find, even if you are hunting for them.

Disturbance and garden maintenance

We have already seen that only a few of our butterflies spend the winter with us as adults, the rest over-wintering as tiny caterpillars or pupae. Only the painted lady and red admiral return to the Continent if they can in the autumn, to warmer habitats. This means that once butterflies have started to use our gardens, we will have to give some thought to the kinds of places they may be during the winter months, and look after the garden accordingly. The next two chapters have information on maintaining specific areas for butterflies, including nectar borders and meadows, and Chapter 6 looks at the garden in winter and how we can help our butterflies survive this inhospitable time.

In general though we have to get used to the idea of tidying the garden less in autumn and winter. This attitude benefits all wildlife in lots of different ways. Many creatures spend the winter months in gardens tucked away in secluded places in borders or around shrubs. Ladybirds congregate inside the dead hollow stems of herbaceous plants or in the dense foliage of evergreens. In my garden hedgehogs often make hibernation nests in the borders beneath the mounds of the dead foliage of hardy geraniums, or under the furry leaves of Verbascum plants. Leaving dead stems and seed heads means that seed eating birds such as finches are able to find natural food in the cold weather, and other birds like wrens and robins will search out insects amongst all this vegetation. It also gives structure to the garden through the winter, providing lots of visual interest especially after frost or snow. If these areas are cut back in autumn, if all soil is exposed, if every bit of long grass is chopped off, then the caterpillars or pupae of butterflies, as well as all those other useful creepy crawlies, will be disturbed and will probably not survive. Those adults that over-winter generally do so in dense vegetation such as ivy, or tuck themselves behind loose bark on fences or tree trunks, although peacocks and small tortoiseshells in particular like to find their way into sheds and outbuildings. All this means that lack of disturbance in the winter garden is crucial. And on the positive side, it gives you an excuse not to go out in the cold weather to tidy up. That job is best done in early March, when things are bursting into life.

Throughout the year, try to keep your garden a safe place for butterflies. Think about the gardening you do and how it might affect them in every stage of their life cycle.

FOUR
Growing Nectar Plants

Most books on gardening for butterflies have lots of plans and designs for butterfly gardens or special nectar borders, but most of us don't have the luxury of starting from scratch in this way. This chapter will concentrate on adapting what you already have in your garden, and incorporating good butterfly nectar plants into your existing borders or wilder spaces. Most really good butterfly gardens are not wildernesses governed by neglect, but instead have a cottage garden feel to them – an attractive and very English style that most gardeners enjoy. There are several good butterfly plants, including some wild flowers that can be grown in containers and will attract butterflies to patios or tiny gardens. This means that helping our native butterflies is something anyone can do, even in the smallest space.

General rules for butterfly nectar plants

Garden Centres have caught on, to some extent at least, to the desire that many 'average' gardeners now have to attract butterflies to their gardens. This has resulted in many of them labelling some species and varieties as 'butterfly plants'. Sadly, some of them have not done their homework! Whether a butterfly feeds from a flower or not depends on two quite simple things. Firstly the flower must produce nectar in sufficient quantity to make it worthwhile for the butterfly to use up energy visiting that plant. Secondly the nectar must be accessible. As far as the first condition is concerned, many plants don't produce any useful nectar. In general these are varieties that have been heavily 'improved' by breeding for flower colour, size of bloom or number of petals. Sometimes this breeding process means that there are more petals but no nectaries, the small organs where nectar is produced in a flower. So one general rule to follow is that double flowered plants often are not attractive to any insects but especially not to butterflies. This is why lists of good butterfly plants often specify 'wild type' or 'true species'. However, there are no hard and fast rules and there will always be plants that defy logic!

The accessibility of the nectar is crucial. Where the flower is composed of many tiny tube-shaped flowers, like Buddleia, the nectar forms and collects in the bottom of the tube until there is a nice little reservoir of sweet sticky syrup. As long as the butterfly has a long enough tongue to reach it, it will feed. Even daisy type flowers like Erigeron or Aster have this flower structure although it is not immediately obvious. The tubes are tiny and packed tightly together. Other examples of this type of flower are Echinacea (coneflower) and scabious – pull one apart sometime and you will find it is composed of many tiny flowers or florets. The smaller the butterfly the shorter its tongue, so tiny butterflies like the common blue are unable to feed on flowers like Buddleia because the tube is too deep, but they can reach the nectar in the florets of a cornflower. It is worth remembering that butterflies do not eat pollen, so flowers like poppies, which have lots of accessible pollen, will be excellent for bees and hoverflies, but will not attract butterflies unless they also have nectar.

So once you have started your collection of butterfly nectar plants, where should they go? Sun is obviously crucial, so the sunniest spot in the garden is a good idea. Small plants such as marjoram or dwarf lavender can go in containers on a patio if you are short of space; larger plants like Michaelmas daisy or coneflower can be added to existing borders in full sun. Try to put a few plants of the same type together – these will be more obvious to passing insects both from their scent and the splash of colour they provide. How much nectar these plants produce will depend on many factors including the weather, the dampness of the soil, and how much sun they get. There are lots of factors involved, and of course one of them is how many butterflies you have around. If you don't see many at all have a look at the Garden Butterfly Year on Page 2. It may simply be a time of year when the first brood of many species has gone, and the second has not yet emerged.

To summarise, here are a few very general rules to help you choose and position nectar plants for butterflies.

◆ Single flowers are better than doubles.
◆ Pale flowers, or mauve, purple or pink flowers are often good.
◆ Flowers should be in sunny spots.
◆ Flowers should be planted in blocks where possible.
◆ Flowers with an obvious tube-type structure often hold more nectar.
◆ Choose plants that flower at different times, especially some for spring and others that continue into the autumn.
◆ Try to grow as many different known nectar plants as possible – as many as 30 if you can find the space. This increases the numbers of butterfly species in the garden enormously.

Best of all when choosing plants, keep a small notebook handy and jot down the names of butterfly attracting plants that you see when you are at Garden Centres, or in a friend's garden or visiting gardens that are open to the public, especially around your own area. Rely on what you see, rather than what you read.

The gatekeeper or hedge brown

Common blue 'roosting' in meadow
grass in the early morning

Wild vervain with a small white

Small coppers are very attracted
to the flowers of wild marjoram

A meadow brown taking nectar
from wild yarrow

A comma basking in the sunshine

The caterpillars of the peacock
butterfly feeding on nettles

An area of long grass and ox eye daisies
left unmown in sunny corner

Two important butterfly
'weeds' - nettles and dandelions

Bird's foot
trefoil and ox eye
daisies amongst
some wild grasses,
including Yorkshire
fog, in a garden
butterfly meadow

Maintenance of nectar plants

Once you have established some nectar plants you will need to think about how to look after them. The previous chapter on making your garden butterfly friendly will give you some guidelines, but there are one or two other factors to consider. Dead-heading will keep your plants flowering for longer. Mulching with a good home made compost, farm yard manure or an organic mulch from the Garden Centre will keep the plants healthy and free from disease, and keeping them well watered (with rain water from a water butt if possible) can prolong flowering.

Growing wild flowers in borders

Some of the best nectar plants you can grow for butterflies are native wild flowers, and here we need to think about where these should go. There is absolutely no reason not to grow some of the best nectar plants amongst non-natives in borders or containers. It is simply a question of choosing wisely and treating them the same as you would any other plant. The list on the centre pages includes some that are suitable for growing in these situations. There are plenty of good wild flowers that will be too vigorous even for the herbaceous border, and these are shown as suitable for a 'wild patch'.

Making a special nectar border

If you have space in your garden you can of course make a special butterfly border using a mixture of the recommended plants on the list in the centre pages. Choose a really sunny area of the garden if you can, and prepare the soil well by removing perennial weeds and adding organic compost. Simply select some shrubs from the list for the very back (preferably on the northern side) to give height and shelter, and then intermingle wild flowers, cottage garden plants and herbs in the area in front of the shrubs. There is really no mystery to designing a border like this. Think a little bit about the colours you like, and place plants with those flower colours next to each other to create some areas where the colours blend together, or go for extreme contrasts like purple next to orange. Try to select plants that flower in the spring, summer and autumn and if you like, include a few caterpillar food plants selected from those listed in the centre pages.

As far as looking after your border is concerned, disturb it as little as possible in the autumn and winter, and cut back dead growth and prune Buddleias hard in early spring. Mulch at this time when the soil is damp – this will suppress weeds as well as feed the plants, keeping them healthy and strong.

FIVE
Growing Larval Food Plants

Larval or caterpillar food plants are the species on which our butterflies (and moths) lay their eggs, and the leaves (or sometimes the flower buds, or seed pods), are eaten by the caterpillars when they hatch. In general these plants are wild flowers or shrubs as you would expect, but some butterflies have adapted to laying their eggs on non-native plants which are similar to those they normally use. An example of a versatile butterfly is the orange tip, normally using the leaves of lady's smock (also called cuckoo flower) for its caterpillars, but happy to lay its eggs on honesty or sweet rocket, both plants from the same family as lady's smock, but not native to Britain. These alternative plants are very useful to the butterfly gardener, as they are often very attractive garden flowers in their own right as well as plants that encourage certain butterfly species to breed. In the list of larval food plants on the centre pages, those that are not native are indicated.

Assuming that we wish butterflies to breed in our gardens, and this is obviously the most practical way that gardeners can contribute to their conservation, we need to be able to incorporate these food plants into the garden in an attractive way. Some are perfect in borders or even containers (bird's foot trefoil is a good example for the latter) and can be grown in quite small gardens, whereas others, like garlic mustard, can be tucked under a hedge bottom if you find them less interesting, where they will establish and self seed. I tend to let several of these caterpillar food plants seed and spread wherever they will in my garden, because the more opportunities there are for butterflies to breed, the more adults I will have feeding on the summer flowers. The list on the centre pages gives an idea of some good locations for them, and it is important to remember that for most a sunny spot is necessary.

Maintenance of larval food plants
The maintenance of these plants is crucial. There is obviously no point in growing them only to chop off the vital bits when the caterpillars are feeding on them! The majority of the time, you won't be able to find the butterfly larvae or pupae because they are very adept at camouflage, so in general you won't know if they are there or not. The only exceptions are the very conspicuous small tortoiseshell and peacock caterpillars. These can be quite apparent on the leaves of nettles, often all together in a tent of silken threads.

So on the whole, it is just a question of leaving well alone, and tidying up the plants a little in the early spring along with your nectar plants. Don't be tempted to pull out sweet rocket, honesty or garlic mustard when they are setting seed - caterpillars of the orange tip or green veined white could be hiding amongst the seed pods which they closely resemble. The only active maintenance you need to consider is to cut back nettles, if you grow them, in late June or early July, first checking that there are no caterpillars. Once the first brood of peacocks or small tortoiseshells has hatched, pupated, and the new batch of butterflies produced, these fresh adults prefer to lay their eggs on nice young nettle leaves, which will spring up if you cut the plants back at this time.

Meadow butterflies

It is relatively easy in most gardens to attract a selection of our most beautiful butterflies, such as painted lady, small tortoiseshell, red admiral and peacock. They will feed on nectar plants that we provide for them, especially Buddleia, and with some thoughtful planning we can also tempt them to breed. There are a few other species we may see, like the migrant clouded yellow that may pass through in good years. But so far there is one group of butterflies that we haven't mentioned. These are the species that lay their eggs on native grasses, often in meadows or perhaps on the grasses on the sunny side of a hedgerow. The life cycles and food preferences of these butterfly species indicate just how important long grass of some sort is to these insects in the countryside. But with the right conditions, some of them can be encouraged to our gardens to breed and stay around if we supply them with their larval food plants – native grasses. They include the gatekeeper, speckled wood, marbled white, ringlet, meadow brown, small and large skipper, small heath and wall brown. This sounds like a gardener's dream. Caterpillars that mow the grass for us! But of course it is nothing like that. These are meadow butterflies that have very specific breeding requirements and one of these is that the grasses their caterpillars eat must be kept relatively long and undisturbed. The other important consideration is that the average rye grass lawn will not do. The best way of making a home for these butterflies is to create a wildflower meadow containing a selection of several different species of native grasses.

Making a wildflower meadow

Wildflower meadows have become very popular in recent years, in both large and small gardens. They look wonderful, reduce work in the garden, and of course attract a wide range of wildlife - not just the butterflies we are interested in but insects of all types, small mammals and birds.

Garden meadows should always be in full sun if possible. Although it is perfectly possible to create an area of wildflowers and grass in light shade, for instance under fruit trees as I have, more butterflies will be attracted to sunnier spots. It is important to consider your soil type before you embark on a project such as a meadow. In good, rich soil a meadow will not establish well. The grass may grow too vigorously and swamp the wildflowers. There must be no perennial weeds such as thistles or couch grass (although thistles in a little wild patch are good butterfly nectar plants). So thought and preparation are needed and there will be hard work involved.

If you feel you have a suitable spot for a wildflower meadow, the area must first be prepared. If there is turf, it must be stripped off, unless it is very thin, patchy and composed of native species. If you think this might be the case, it is best to consult one of the books on the inside back cover and follow directions about enhancing an existing grassy area, but bear in mind it is just about impossible to do this with modern rye grass lawns. In general you will need to start from scratch and possibly hire a turf cutter if the area is large. If your soil is very fertile, it may be necessary to remove this to a depth of 30 cms and replace it with something poorer – the soil from the bottom of a hole where a pond is to be installed, is often ideal. If you are removing turf from an area where the grass has been neglected, never fertilised but repeatedly mown year after year, then the soil quality should be suitable for a garden meadow.

Next the perennial weeds need to be dealt with. If the area is small, digging out thistle, nettle, ground elder and couch roots is the organic alternative. If you can think well ahead, covering the area with thick black polythene to exclude light for a few months will also achieve the desired result. If you have no objection to using herbicides then something like Roundup, which breaks down on contact with the soil, can be used.

The best time to sow meadow seed is early spring, but autumn will also produce a good result. There are several specialist seed growers producing native grass and wildflower mixes, (see inside back cover) and it is vital to ensure that the seeds are of native origin. It is also important to choose a mixture that suits your own soil. Do you have clay, or sand or chalky soil? Is it well drained or waterlogged? Wildflowers can be fussy about the soil conditions they grow in, and if you plant inappropriate species for your soil type they will quickly disappear. Your seed supplier will have a range of mixes suitable for all soil types. You will need to roughly calculate the area you have and sow a seed mixture at a rate of about 4 grams per square meter.

Hopefully you are starting with soil that is weed free and not too fertile. It should be broken down into a fine tilth, and the seed scattered on to the soil surface as evenly as you can. The best course of action is to then walk up and down on the area, pressing the seed into the soil with your feet or use a garden roller. It is not necessary to cover the seed up – in fact excluding light can hinder germination of some native wildflowers. When sowing is complete, water well if the conditions are dry, and protect the seed from birds. The most effective way of doing this is to hang a few old, shiny CD's around the area, to sparkle and catch the light. This always seems to work really well in my garden, and I have lots of birds around!

The grass will germinate quickly depending on the weather conditions, and some of the wildflower species will also appear quite quickly. Others, especially cowslips, will not germinate until they have had a period of cold frosty weather, so if you sow in the springtime, you will not see these until the following year. Over time, new species will appear, and you can also expect some germination of seeds that have lain dormant in your own soil, sometimes for many years.

Your meadow will need basic annual maintenance. It must be cut at least once every year in the late summer or autumn, and the hay raked off thoroughly in order to maintain the conditions that the wildflowers require. But we must ensure that the grass is not cut too short or we may be exposing the butterfly caterpillars and pupae that could be resting down in the short turf over the winter months. In general, cutting your meadow to between 5 and 10 cms will keep these insects safe from the worst of the weather and from predators – although of course a certain amount of predation from birds, hedgehogs and other insects is quite natural and must be expected.

If you are a real enthusiast your meadow maintenance can be much more complicated. Parts of the meadow can be cut at different times to encourage specific butterfly species to breed, but in general the keen gardener can contribute to the breeding success of the meadow butterflies with just the basic upkeep outlined above.

Adding more species to your butterfly meadow

As long as you have sown a seed mixture from a reputable supplier, it will contain the essential grass species for some of the meadow butterflies. If you have any doubt, check the list of species in your seed mix with the list of larval food plants on the centre pages. If the specific types of grass are not included, go to another supplier. One useful addition you can make to your meadow, once it is established, is to add small plants or plugs of other larval food plants, or special nectar plants to really give the butterflies plenty of options. I always try to add extra larval food plants including bird's foot trefoil for the common blue, sorrel for the small copper and then a few more good nectar plants for the adults – field scabious, greater knapweed and especially wild marjoram. It can make the meadow look a bit 'top heavy' with flowers, but the objective here is to make a good habitat for butterflies, rather than try to recreate a proper wild meadow which would never be possible. What we are doing here is making a 'meadow effect', and if you want it to have lots of flowers, it's up to you. If you have decided that a small meadow in your garden is something you would like to try, make sure you read the information on making meadows in one of the books recommended on the inside back cover.

So it is quite possible for the average gardener to contribute to the survival of some of our prettiest butterflies by catering for their caterpillars' needs in the garden. With some larval food plants in your borders or containers, and maybe a little meadow area in a sunny spot, you will find that both the numbers and species of butterfly in your garden will soon start to rise.

SIX

The Winter Garden

Throughout this booklet the hibernation of butterflies has been frequently mentioned and it stands to reason that for these insects to be with us year after year, they must get through the cold winter months in some form or another. A few hibernate as adult butterflies, and most of us have come across a peacock or small tortoiseshell butterfly flapping against the window of a garden shed or garage on a mild and sunny winter's day. Others survive the winter as tiny caterpillars, waiting for warmer weather before they continue to feed on their larval food plant, or as pupae in suspended animation. These butterflies emerge as fully-grown adults when the conditions are right for them.

Finding butterflies in the winter

We are unlikely to see a caterpillar or pupa outside during the winter months – they are usually tucked away safely and difficult to find and as long as the garden is not over tidied, they can be left to themselves. We can be more positively helpful to the species that over-winter as adults by providing them with shelter.

Firstly, what should we do with a butterfly in the garage or shed on a sunny winter's day? If the weather is relatively warm early in the year, a butterfly can be let out to find a new more suitable hibernation place. Sometimes butterflies find their way into the house in the autumn, and choose an out-of-the-way spot in a bedroom or other cool room, for hibernation. They may wake up because the room warms up. Putting them outside in freezing weather would almost certainly finish them off. In this situation it is best to relocate them to a cool but frost-free shed, where hopefully they will return to hibernation unharmed. Unfortunately, any butterfly coming out of hibernation early has a problem, in that it will have used up some of its stored food reserves, but there will be very little or no nectar around for it outside.

The more good hibernation places you have outside for butterflies, the less likely they are to come into the house, and find themselves in this situation. They will find dry places in log piles, under flakes of bark on tree stumps, in the overlap in larch lap fencing or sometimes in cracks in walls. One of the best hibernation spots for adult butterflies, especially brimstones and commas, is amongst climbing vegetation on walls. Ivy is particularly good for this purpose.

Here are a few ideas to help you help your butterflies through the winter months:

Helping Butterflies through the Winter

◆ Make sure you have early flowering nectar plants, especially dandelions.
◆ Leave ivy and other thick climbing plants against walls, undisturbed.
◆ Create log piles or wood piles, or leave dead tree stumps with flaking bark.
◆ Leave all herbaceous plants alone until the early spring.
◆ Cut meadows in the autumn to no less that 5 cms and then leave undisturbed through the winter.
◆ Try to leave a few small areas of long grass completely uncut through the autumn and winter, and cut them in the spring-time.

These measures will help all sorts of wildlife in your garden, not just butterflies.

In Conclusion

Butterflies can enhance our enjoyment of gardens tremendously. Even the most beautiful garden, devoid of these lovely colourful insects will seem less interesting and alive. As we continue to lose good butterfly habitat from our countryside, anyone with a garden, however small, can make a valuable contribution to the conservation of some of our native butterfly species by creating a habitat for them in their own little nature reserve outside the back door. Grow some of the plants they need, provide them with shelter and all the other wildlife visiting your garden will benefit too.